SILVER CREEK

River Journal

Volume 1, Number 2, 1993

About The Author

David Joye spent the major part of his life as a "normal" human in the Southern California area in quest of the elusive buck. After finally realizing that there were more important things to chase, such as wily trout, he retreated to the banks of the Big Wood River in Ketchum, Idaho, where he now resides.

David has fished Silver Creek since 1968, and guided fly fishing trips there off-and-on for the better part of ten years. He is also a freelance writer with credits in *Flyfishing*, *Sun Valley Magazine* and *Western Outdoors*. Nature/Outdoor photography is his other "serious" hobby.

◆

Acknowledgments

Many thanks to: Paul Todd of the Silver Creek Preserve for current information on the Nature Conservancy; Judy Perry, the smartest, best-looking (sorry guys, she's very happily married) copy editor ever created; and, Outfitters Terry Ring, Scott Schnebly and Bill Mason for letting me pick their brains often.

◆

Series Editor: Jeff Findley

Subscriptions: Softbound, $30.00 for one year (four issues), $55.00 for two years. Hardbound limited editions, $80.00 one year, $150.00 for two years.

Design: Joyce Herbst • Typesetting: Charlie Clifford
Fly Plates: Jim Schollmeyer • Map: Tony Amato
All Photos: W. David Joye unless otherwise noted.
Printed in Hong Kong
ISBN: Softbound 1-878175-33-5, Hardbound 1-878175-34-3

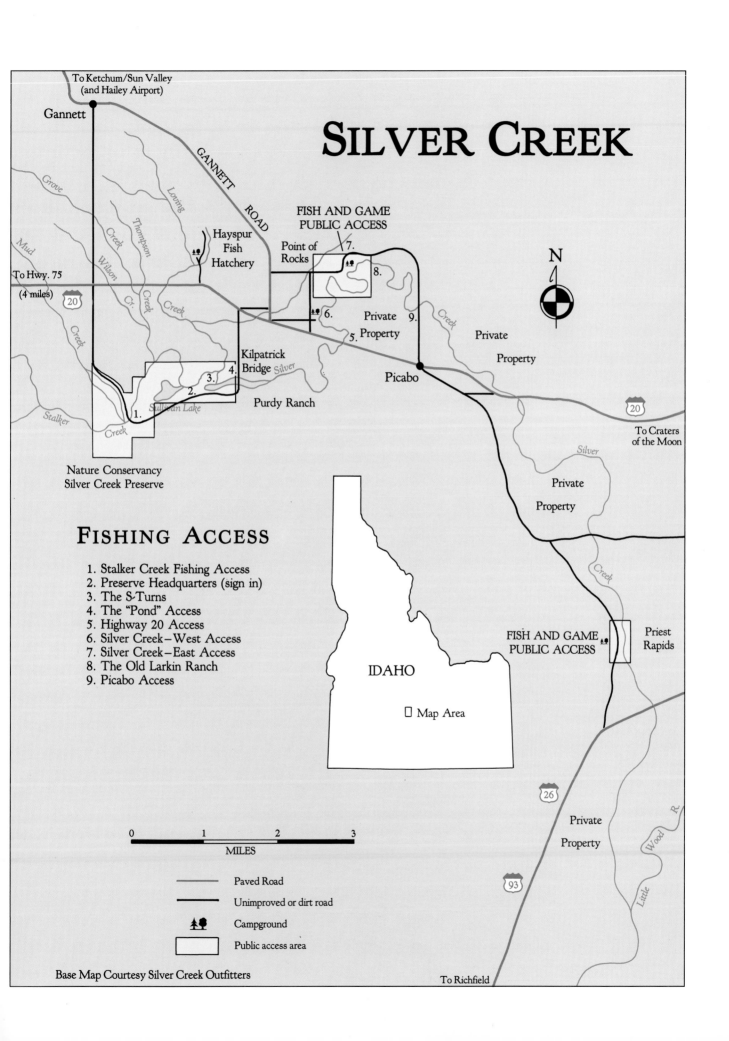

SILVER CREEK

To Ketchum/Sun Valley
(and Hailey Airport)

Gannett

GANNETT ROAD

Grove

Loving

Thompson

Creek

Wilson Cr.

Mud

To Hwy. 75
(4 miles)

20

Creek

Creek

Stalker

Creek

Hayspur
Fish
Hatchery

FISH AND GAME
PUBLIC ACCESS

Point of
Rocks

7.

8.

6.

5.

Private
Property

9.

Creek

Private
Property

N

Kilpatrick
Bridge

Silver

3.   4.

2.

1.

Sullivan Lake

Purdy Ranch

Picabo

20

To Craters
of the Moon

Silver

Nature Conservancy
Silver Creek Preserve

Private
Property

FISHING ACCESS

1. Stalker Creek Fishing Access
2. Preserve Headquarters (sign in)
3. The S-Turns
4. The "Pond" Access
5. Highway 20 Access
6. Silver Creek—West Access
7. Silver Creek—East Access
8. The Old Larkin Ranch
9. Picabo Access

IDAHO

☐ Map Area

Creek

FISH AND GAME
PUBLIC ACCESS

Priest
Rapids

0   1   2   3

MILES

26

Private
Property

Wood R.

93

Little

———— Paved Road

———— Unimproved or dirt road

🏕 Campground

▭ Public access area

Base Map Courtesy Silver Creek Outfitters

To Richfield

Ketchum resident Earl Cohen cradles nice brown taken with Woolly Bugger in October.

SILVER CREEK

◆

*A*FRONT MOVED DOGGEDLY OVER THE CAMAS PRAIRIE from the west, taking dead-aim on the little valley in south-central Idaho where a spring-fed stream called Silver Creek meanders among fields of potatoes, grain and white-faced heifers.

Ominous black clouds hovered overhead, and the two fly fishermen, waist-deep in the stream, hastily pulled rain jackets over their heads in anticipation of what was to come. Wind gusts lashed at the four-weight lines and 7X-tippets they threw. A sudden clash of thunder announced the arrival of the rain, which soon turned to sleet, and then to hail, making the water's surface a sea of spattered dimples. Against this clattering backdrop the two anglers moved closer together, shouting to be heard above the rowdy elements.

"Great day, huh?", offered the grinning, shorter man with the Chicago Cubs cap and chewing tobacco-stained lips.

"Perfect!", replied his older, taller partner sporting an oil-skin rain jacket past due for retirement to the Fly Fishing Museum of Angling Memorabilia.

With hailstones ricocheting wildly off the brim of his cap, the Cubbies fan reached deep into his vest, beyond the no-hackle/midge box, and produced a weathered and beaten pewter flask that had obviously been party to many such rituals.

"Here, this'll help melt any hail you've swallowed". His friend accepted the offer with blue-white hands, gestured in the direction of his benefactor, then enjoyed a long swill of sour-mash from the icy container. He continued the ceremony by passing the flask back to its owner, who proceeded to melt several hailstones of his own.

Waddling and sloshing back to the car, they chortled as they went, humbled this day by the weather, not by the fish. Another chapter in the book of Silver Creek had been logged.

Oh, there had been fish briefly taken, one of them a decent 16-inch brown, fat from a summer of gorging bugs and things. But more than the fish and the fishing on this most pleasant of streams, it is the sum of the parts; something esoteric that makes days like these momorable...*sui generis*. How else can we explain to normal humans the appeal of such times for two seemingly lucid, middle-aged males? If one needs clarification, in all probability they won't understand even if you give them your very best "why". It has always been thus with fly-fisher-people, and for those who accept the many challenges of Silver Creek, the list of "whys" can be incredibly long and confounding.

Captivating And Capricious . . .
A Glorious Paradox

SILVER CREEK IS A SEDUCTIVE AND ENCHANTED princess. She inveigles her followers with alluring curves, a gentleness that belies her fickle demeanor, and a warped sense of fair play. Her constituency is comprised of a large population of splendid trout, each a clone of Her Highness, beautiful, but contrary. Yet, in spite of the frustrations and regardless of recurrent foibles, Silver Creek's disciples queue up early and often to seek her favor. Though commonly disgruntled and disappointed, rarely are they disheartened; they return day after day, year after year for more epic servings of humble pie.

Because of Silver Creek's fame throughout the entire domain of fishing with the long-rod, feathers and fur, favored runs must periodically be shared from July 4th through September. But for the balance of the fishing year the pleasures of tranquil solitude are the norm, not the exception.

Vacationers staying in nearby Sun Valley often want to sample Idaho's legendary dry-fly fishing, and will book a guided fly-fishing trip for the day. For some, the only fly-stream they have heard of, via books and well-meaning friends, is Silver Creek, and that is where a few of these novices ask to be taken. Fortunately, for all parties concerned, the guide and/or outfitter convinces most of them of the folly of their request. Long-time Silver Creek guide and outfitter Scott Schnebly, suggests for those he deems not-ready-for-primetime: "To fish Silver Creek the first time out with a fly rod is like playing golf at Augusta National the first time out with golf clubs." Without heeding this advice, multi-digit scores would be recorded in Georgia, no-digit scores at Silver Creek.

No doubt at all that Silver Creek is a tough venue for the fly fisherman. A long and fruitless day of watching those gnarly dark heads, dorsal fins and paint-brush tails bulge the surface will firmly convince you of that. If you feel obliged to reach out and smack a fish with your rod tip, you won't be the first. Boiling trout will often swamp your fly as they rise for a natural floating side-by-side. Refusal is a way of life here, and anglers with sensitive egos will probably not enjoy the experience. But all this should not discourage the serious neophyte from pitting his or her modest skills against the always-finicky, sometimes-belligerent Silver Creek trout.

◆

Mule deer graze in safety at far western end of preserve near Sullivan Lake.

Hopefully, the following pages will provide some assistance in coping with the conditions encountered on the stream. Hold the thought, however, that some pretty adept fly casters have taken advance courses in "Learning Humility" from this venerable trout fishing place. It comes with the territory. A frequent comment is heard from anglers departing the creek with furrowed brows, "Well, (sigh) Silver Creek wins again." It is one of the few contests in the sporting life where there is really no such thing as losing. The rewards of success on Silver Creek are great and the temporary "setbacks" are shared by the multitude who have passed this turbid way before.

Averill Builds A Ski Resort . . . And Uncovers A Treasure

IN THE FALL OF 1935, AVERILL HARRIMAN, THEN Chairman of Union Pacific Railway, had recently returned from Europe where Alpine skiing was flourishing in the posh Austrian, Swiss and French Alps. The United States had no such facilities then and the far-sighted Harriman sought to change that.

Because his railroad was without any of the famous tourist attractions served by his competition, Harriman hoped that the ideal site for America's first-ever luxury ski resort could be found within a short distance of an existing UP railhead from which he would then transport skiers to the slopes. To research and oversee the selection of such a perfect setting, Harriman enlisted the aid of Count Felix Schaffgotsch, an Austrian skier of some nobility whom Harriman had met earlier in New York and who knew well the requirements for a first class mountain.

The Count's quest led him to potential ski mountains throughout the West: in Washington, California, Oregon, Utah, Colorado, Wyoming, and ultimately Idaho. In December of 1935, the Count stepped off a train in the town of Shoshone, Idaho, and into a raging blizzard. The 60 mile drive to Ketchum in blinding snow was completed in total darkness. It is said that the Count awakened in Ketchum to two feet of fresh powder snow and a bright, crisp Idaho winter morning. The steep, resplendent mountains surrounding the Wood River Valley glistened in the warm sun and Schaffgotsch knew his search had ended.

Averill Harriman arrived in February to finalize the deal, and in March of 1936, Union Pacific announced the purchase of 3,888 acres for $39,000, $10.04 per acre. Harriman had found the perfect spot for his soon-to-be legendary ski resort. All that remained to be done, aside from the obvious construction, was to give the place a name that would forever inspire visions of all the resort hoped it would become. That was a cinch, and Sun Valley opened for business during the gala Christmas of 1936.

chosen to build his ski area smack in the middle of one of the truly great trout-fishing regions God had ever created. No doubt Harriman had been apprised of the fabulous fishing sometime during the acquisition and construction period in 1936, but there is no indication that the fishing had any bearing at all on the final decision to put the resort where he did.

The "discovery" of Silver Creek as a bonus to the resort came about as a result of Sun Valley's public relations whiz Steve Hannagan. It was Hannagan's job to put the new resort on the map by coaxing, or otherwise bribing, the stars of stage, screen and radio in Hollywood to come and frolic in the snow in Sun Valley (where?), Idaho (where?). A scant few of the Tinsel town celebs actually skied well, but no one cared too much about their athletic abilities. All of the PR shots would be stills, and with the right outfits, practically everyone looked good standing on the side of a ski run or riding the worlds first chair lift. Sun Valley became an over-night sensation, the place to be to slide down the mountain with Claudette Colbert, Lowell Thomas, Clark Gable, Joan Bennett and countless other headliners of the day. But the ski season was short; Christmas through April at the longest, and the huge and luxurious Sun Valley Lodge could be left empty the remaining eight months of the year. That much of a vacancy factor just wouldn't "pencil" and it posed problems such as re-staffing.

That was probably the gist of the conversation between Harriman and Steve Hannagan quite soon after that first winter. "How can we get people to come here after the snow melts?", surely must have been the question asked by all concerned.

◆

This sign is seen at entrances to the Silver Creek Preserve of the Nature Conservancy. Welcome and Enjoy.

The front porch of the Nature Conservancy headquarters cabin overlooking the creek. The sign-in book is to the right. Here you may pick up preserve regulations, information, souvenir t-shirts, and Silver Creek flies you forgot to bring. Open in summer only, although Paul Todd, preserve manager, will many times be found there at any time of year.

◆

So it was that Hannagan invited the world's most famous writer-hunter-outdoorsman, Ernest Hemingway, to come and sample some of Idaho's hunting and fishing, and the word would quickly spread among outdoor writers and enthusiasts; Sun Valley was a paradise. It was about then that Hemingway met Gary Cooper. "Papa" and "Coop", a native of Montana and an avid hunter, became lifelong shooting pals as a result. Hemingway wasn't much of a fly fisherman, however, even though he had written fishing classics such as "Big Two-Hearted River" and other well-read Nick Adams tales. The reasoning for Ernest's apathy toward trout fishing with a fly was that at this stage of his life he was addicted to the raptures of taking giant tuna and black marlin in the salt. A three or four pound trout simply didn't tax his strength and virility. But Hemingway dearly loved to hunt, and the fields and woods surrounding Sun Valley abounded with chukar, grouse, pheasant, deer and elk. The writer accepted Hannagan's invitation, arriving at the Lodge in September of 1939, and staying until December 9th. Hemingway liked what he saw. Liked it so well in fact that he returned nearly every autumn for the next twenty years.

Hemingway was also told of the terrific duck and goose hunting on a placid spring creek about 25 or 30 miles south of Sun Valley. Silver Creek it was called, and he visited the creek often when staying in the valley, frequently taking his young son "Bumby" along. Years later, Jack Hemingway, having outgrown the childhood nickname, would spend much of his adult life living in the revered Wood River

Valley of his youth. The younger Hemingway's presence in Sun Valley would also have a major impact on the long term prognosis for Silver Creek.

By 1964, Union Pacific had run its course as operators of America's Granddaddy of all ski resorts. One era ended and another began when California skier/real estate developer Bill Janss purchased all Union Pacific holdings in Sun Valley for $3,000,000. An important part of that transaction, for fly fishermen in particular, was the inclusion of the land surrounding that wonderful spring creek where Ernest Hemingway had shot ducks 25 years earlier. In 1975, Janss, too, was ready to move on to other endeavors, and he began looking around for someone to buy him out, including the priceless Silver Creek parcel.

Jack Hemingway sensed that here was an opportunity to secure the future of a precious ecological resource, and he quickly organized a group to contact the Nature Conservancy. Six months later the Conservancy purchased the original 480 acres of the Silver Creek Preserve, and subsequently retired the debt by raising $500,000 from the private sector of citizens and business. That was only the beginning of great things to come.

Fly fishermen, conservationists, bird lovers, and all naturalists near and far were assured that Silver Creek was forever protected from threats of development and misuse. In the years that have followed, the Conservancy has expanded the scope of operations greatly by making a commitment of more than $3,000,000 to protect over 20 miles of stream and 5,043 acres of Silver Creek habitat and tributaries.

◆

Waterfowl gather by the thousands on Sullivan Lake at the western end of Silver Creek Preserve. This glassy compound is also a haven for some very big cruisers that can be fooled, but only with delicate presentations, light tippets and cautious, kneeling casts from the bank.

Silver Creek Preserve manager, Paul Todd, on his way home from a tough day at the office. Nice job.

A River Of Many Riches

GETTING TWO FLY FISHERMEN TO AGREE ON A TOPIC of discussion, whether it be size, shape and shade of the perfect fly to match the hatch or something so simple as the preferred color of a dry fly line can frequently become a Herculean task. Perhaps it is because our sport is so very subjective a pursuit. Fly anglers of either gender or any age can range from being merely opinionated, to downright snobs. Ask any of them their views on almost anything that pertains to angling with a fly, and the Great Debate pales by comparison.

One of the few exceptions to the widely differing convictions is the general accord found when knowledgeable fly anglers are queried about their choice as the most fertile and prolific spring creek in America. Seldom would any fly-person rank Silver Creek below the top three or four. Those that should know, the fish and game analysts, stream biologists, outdoor writers and university-level fisheries specialists rate this fishery at-or-near the head of

such lists. Small wonder. Silver Creek is extremely rich with mineral nutrients so essential to lush aquatic vegetation. As is common among spring creeks, with the profuse vegetation come the dense hordes of mayflies, caddis and stoneflies. During every month of the calendar, there will be bugs of some variety hatching and feeding the resident trout. Every important hatch will be identified and placed in chronological order in a later segment of this journal.

Silver Creek is an ecologically unique, high-desert cold-spring system formed by springs that rise from underground aquifers. Therefore the water temperatures and levels are quite constant when compared to typical freestone rivers. This consistency of conditions results in nutrient-rich alkaline cold springs providing ideal trout water, rich and cool and constant.

Several smaller feeder creeks with clean, gravel stream bottoms are the nurseries for Silver Creek. Here, spawning and reproduction are near-optimum. What this means to the fly rod angler is perfect trout habitat. Aquatic grasses flourish and food sources are bountiful. Undercut banks provide safe shelter, and generally superb feeding, holding and hiding water exists for even the most fussy of the rivers finny residents. Trout Heaven.

The rainbow, brown and brook trout that are present in Silver Creek are not native to the system, but are the progeny of many generations of wild fish; no fish have been stocked here since 1975. Interestingly, the trout that are thought to have been native, the cutthroat, are no longer found in the river, having been displaced by the aforementioned species. The Rocky Mountain Whitefish is also native to Silver Creek, and although common it is not the pest to dry fly anglers it is in many Western rivers.

Sharing this natural Utopia with its piscatorial neighbors are over 150 species of birds, including bald and golden eagles, sandhill cranes, Canadian honkers, trumpeter swans, a dozen species of ducks, pheasant, songbirds and shorebirds. Mule deer, elk, coyote and a rare mountain lion also frequent the Silver Creek environs.

Perhaps the miracle of all this is that the public is allowed to use and enjoy almost the entire length of river at absolutely no charge. Portions of the land adjoining the creek are private, but even then the waterway itself is considered navigable and may be floated in a canoe or float tube, provided the floater does not trespass beyond the high-water mark.

The Silver Creek Preserve maintains a Visitors' Center with educational displays, merchandise, a nature trail and a knowledgeable staff (during summer). Complete information regarding the Catch-and-Release, barbless hook fly fishing, bird watching, hiking and hunting is available at the center. The preserve relies entirely upon donations to fund its operations.

During its initial year under the flag of the Nature Conservancy, just over a thousand visitors, mostly fly fishermen, came to savor the river's bounty. By 1987 that number had reached a staggering 7,600 visitors for the year. Since that record year, annual visitor figures have

Columbine in many color combinations is an early summer resident throughout the area.

mercifully leveled off at an average of approximately 7,000. About 80-90 percent of that figure are fishermen, and almost half of them line the banks and wade the river during July and August. The impact of that invasion is under study; there is a chance that if visitor counts should again increase sharply, angler quotas and/or some form of limited usage could be imposed.

Fiscal contributions are not the only way to aid in the day-to-day operations of the Silver Creek Preserve. Each summer, and sometimes well into the fall, scores of volunteers become involved in a host of streamside restoration programs ranging from general clean-up to the planting of over 10,000 native shrubs and trees along several of the feeder creeks. The new vegetation will help deter bank erosion and eventually furnish shade to reduce summer heat-up.

The long range effect of this kind of work will coincide with the cattle fencing on these same feeders to substantially lessen the amount of sediments flowing into the main river, and regenerate critical spawning beds throughout the Silver Creek basin.

Without the efforts of the strong corps of volunteers, further improvements by Mother Nature would be painfully slow.

Clearly, the ecological future of Silver Creek lies in the hands of some very dedicated people who sacrifice their time so that the countless anglers who fish here will continue to enjoy their sport to the maximum. Most of the studies, such as a comprehensive water quality monitoring program, the effect of brown trout infiltration of rainbow trout habitat and management of upstream siltation, are conducted under the auspices of the Nature Conservancy, but make no mistake, the entire Silver Creek fishery will benefit from what happens on the preserve.

Big browns ready for spawning in Grove Creek, October.

Floating Down The River

THE EASIEST WAY TO SEE THE ENTIRE LENGTH OF fishable Silver Creek would be to float it in a canoe. That does not mean that drifting a canoe would be the choice for fishing, but for purposes of taking an imaginary cruise, we'll travel on top in first class, maybe with some plump turkey sandwiches and a chilled lager or two.

As our tippy boat rounds each bend and glides through the glassy currents, your tour guide will describe the riffles and runs from Stalker Creek at the western-most end, to the gas stop/market hamlet of Picabo (pronounced, "Peek-a-boo"), a distance of about 15 stream miles. Our journey will take us through many types of water and through some areas of restricted uses like the Nature Conservancy preserve, private land, and, of course, all public access areas.

So put your rod together, tie on some 6X or 7X-tippet and a little Parachute Adams, rub some Cutter's on the back of your neck along with a good bit of sunscreen, and let's shove off.

Silver Creek is basically a west-east current as it gathers quantity from the hundreds of smaller spring creeks originating at the southern end of the wood River Valley and in the pastures below the borough of Gannett. The first section covered will all be within the Silver Creek Preserve of the Nature Conservancy, and visitors must register at the Visitors' Center prior to wetting a line (see map: Visitors' Center).

One of the largest feeder-creeks is Stalker Creek, a rather narrow (20-40 feet in width) and shallow stream with a heavily silted bottom and willow-lined banks. Merging with Silver Creek at the west end of the preserve, the flow of the combined streams is increased substantially. In years gone by, Stalker Creek held a good population of brookies, some in the 14-inch class, but that fishery is not what it once was and Stalker Creek receives little pressure when compared to the assault that occurs a short distance downstream. There is a fisherman's access at the bridge crossing Stalker Creek on the dirt road near the entry to the Silver Creek Preserve from the north (see map: Stalker Creek access). Stalker is the only tributary that is accessible

Jack Perry of Sun Valley about to find out how deep Silver Creek is. Staying on your toes here should be taken literally.

Dr. Connie Stover enjoys a picture-perfect evening on Silver Creek.

to the public, and really the only one that offers angling opportunities. The fishing here should improve greatly as the sedimentation problems upstream are resolved.

Moving with the current from the confluence, the creek winds through willows and among small islands, past the convergence of Grove Creek, for about a mile before reaching the Visitors' Center perched on the side of the hill with a grand overlook of the entire river below. This water doesn't get the angler crush of the runs immediately downstream either, but does present an alternative to the crowds and can fish very well. Guide Jim Miller, on a "Postman's Holiday" caught and released a 27-inch brown trout in this section in the summer of 1990 casting a big Whitlock Hopper tight against the bank where the big brown fella was leisurely gulping anything that came along, probably including mice, slow birds and six-inch rainbows.

From the Visitors' cabin the stream continues its wandering ways, forming a series of channels through islands, producing deep runs and typical Silver Creek trout lies. (author's note: fish lies differ vastly from fishermen's lies.) It is from this point east, i.e., downstream, that fly-rodders have tended to agree is the choicest water on the

preserve. In mid-July the minuscule Tricos come off in swarms, causing large trout to "pod-up" by around eight a.m.. It isn't unusual to find a fly fisherman sipping a cup of coffee from the bank adjacent to his favored run by seven a.m., "guarding" his spot until the fun begins. The Silver Creek Trico hatch is something to see; it's frustrating beyond belief, but a chance to nail some fish with shoulders the size of Dick Butkus.

As we slide along the smooth and shimmering artery, it is easy to understand how the creek acquired its name; it is indeed a silvery ribbon of water. In some areas there appears to be no movement of water whatsoever, but that deceiving vision is quashed as an apparently well-presented Blue Winged Olive quickly drags in the vexing cross-currents. Reading the water here is elevated to an art-form; often the difference between success and failure.

The section from the conservancy cabin to the top of the tubing area is prime trout habitat; there are deep, weed-banded channels, and slick feeding lanes where rainbows of all sizes lie in wait for the endless procession of mayflies, hoppers, ants and caddis that are delivered straight to their dining rooms. Loving Creek enters the main stream in this area and the conflux of the two streams is a dear position to long-time Silver Creek devotees.

Beyond Loving Creek are the demanding S-Turns, or as a thoroughly crestfallen angler was heard to quip late one autumn afternoon, "They ought to rename this spot The S.O.B.-Turns!" Few would disagree who have spent a "lifetime" one day changing flies, lengthening tippets, revising attitudes and creating new and strange casting techniques in an all-out attempt to coax a rise from one of the chunkers (larger than lunkers) who hang out here. Toss in the added dimension of wading in tippy-toed over the tops of your neoprenes, and the challenge of the S-Turns is complete.

At the bottom of the S-Turns the river flattens and widens into a large pond where float tubing is permitted. Without the use of a tube this would be an impossible section to fish due to the depth of the water in some spots and extremely difficult wading conditions in knee-deep gunk in others. The upper portions of this pond can be excellent, given the right conditions, i.e., a slight breeze to put some wrinkles on the otherwise mirrored surface.

Floating through the pond is sometimes a misnomer. If the wind is blowing upstream, as it frequently does, a considerable number of calories will be burned-off slogging through the muck down to the usual point of exit at Kilpatrick Bridge (see map: Kilpatrick Bridge).

The usual method of fishing this section is to park at Kilpatrick Bridge and pack your tube upstream as far as is possible, following a path on the south side of the stream. Enter the water at this point and either plod through the water upstream to the "End of Tubing Area" signs on both sides of the creek, or merely start fishing at the put-in and float back to the bridge. This is a good alternative to those days in July and August when it seems everyone who owns a fly rod in the Western Hemisphere has decided to ply the riffles and runs of Silver Creek, Idaho.

◆

Feisty 17 inch rainbow briefly taken near confluence with Loving Creek.

Ground-hugging blue flax is a mid-summer bonus on the creek.

◆

The Kilpatrick Bridge marks the eastern boundary of the Nature Conservancy water. Although complete regulations are available at the Visitors' Center when signing in for the day's fishing, it should be emphasized that the entire Silver Creek Preserve is restricted to Catch-and-Release fly fishing with barbless hooks only. Reading the brief and informative piece outlining the rules and regs is recommended.

A word or two about entering, exiting and wading Silver Creek. Stepping into the stream can be a wet and exciting event. In fact, merely walking to the bank of the stream is occasionally fraught with peril. Tall grasses and reeds grow profusely in the marshy soil adjoining the river's edge, and this makes visibility of the landing place for your next step poor. The result often means stepping into an unseen, knee-deep pothole followed by a headlong plunge into the glorp. But if no bones are broken in the plunge, this episode will only teach you to walk a bit more carefully next time. "Look before you leap", has never held more meaning.

The experience of a haughty and carefree entrance or step into this creek is one that may never be forgotten by the unwary angler. Unlike typical freestone rivers, there are few beaches of gravel conveniently and gradually deepening as they move from the shore toward the center of the stream. Spring creeks, and this one is a touchstone, can be two to four feet in depth immediately next to the bank-side. Under the several feet of water there also might be a foot or two of ooze or perhaps another sloping bank of slick, hard mud. Any of the above combinations are not going to make for a delicate and graceful, nor dry, entry into the water. To achieve a dry launch, carefully approach the stream, sit down on the bank and let both legs hang into the water. Now slide your rear down the bank slowly until both feet are firmly in position to stand and wade. If it seems too deep and/or too mucky, do a reverse butt-wiggle back up the bank, find a more opportune locale and re-launch.

Belly-boater Jim Croul fast to a nice fish in the pond above Kilpatrick Bridge on Nature Conservancy water.

◆

Exiting a spring creek is not quite so easy as it sounds either. Attempting to take one giant step completely out of the water can result in the always-tough "Back Half-Gainer in the Semi-Tuck Position", a very low-scoring and soggy maneuver. To avoid this, wade to the bank, put your rod on the ground and crawl on your hands and knees out of the water, using handfuls of streamside vegetation to help pull yourself out, if available. Simple but effective ways to truly be a dry fly fishermen.

Wading Silver Creek safely and effectively is more a matter of good judgment than anything else. To wade safely, always respect the river. If you wear chest-high waders other than neoprene, be certain to secure a safety belt around your waist. It is almost a guarantee that you will wade a bit deeper than the tops of your waders on most days of fishing here. There are pools that are well over six feet in depth, and silted stream bottoms that require Olympian strength in order to extract boots and waders. (Note: Except for the warmest days of summer, neoprene waders are the choice of most Silver Creek regulars. Hip boots are far too restrictive, and wading wet is not recommended due to the presence of leeches in the water. [see: "The African Queen", Humphrey Bogart]).

◆

Preceding page: The pond below Kilpatrick Bridge is belly-boat paradise. Free-rising rainbow and brown trout are abundant and large. And hard to fool.

Effective, and careful wading is paramount to duping trout with a fly on this smoothly gliding stream. Terry Ring, owner of Silver Creek Outfitters in Ketchum, and a 20 year authority on the ways of Silver Creek trout, has an opinion on the subject. According to Terry, "The one single reason for the failures of the majority of good fly fishermen on the Creek is sloppy wading. These fish are extremely sensitive to underwater motions and noise. Their sonar is very highly developed, and they pick up the vibrations of the waves caused by careless wading." He continues to make his point, "Poor presentations and bad fly selections are also reasons for disappointment, but mostly by novices. Experienced fly casters usually do everything right until they wade like hippos in a hot tub. That will invariably put the trout under a bank." Wade softly and carry a long rod.

The Purdy Ranch

NOW THAT WE HAVE DRIFTED THROUGH THE FIRST SEGment of Silver Creek and portaged around Kilpatrick Bridge (don't ever attempt to float under this bridge in a tube, canoe, surfboard or anything), it's time to snap a tin and enjoy your turkey sandwich; we've still got miles of water ahead.

From the bridge downstream to the Idaho Highway 20 crossing, Silver Creek snakes its way on a long and magnificent passage through privately owned land known as the

Purdy Ranch. To be correct, the ranch is officially named the Double R Ranch, but it is seldom called that by local folks. Owned by Bud and Ruth Purdy, as it has been since before Papa Hemingway hunted it a half century ago, the ranch contains some of the finest fly fishing water in the contiguous 48 states. There are two ways to fish this part of the creek. One can be among the privileged few (estimated to be about 300) who have been granted membership in a "club" with fishing access-rights to come on the property and throw flies at the enormous population of big brown and rainbow trout who call this place home. A good portion of the members at Purdy's are from out-of-state, or, at the very least, out-of-the-area, in order to keep angling pressure at a comfortable level. Were all members local residents, the demand upon the better runs could become a problem. As is, only those periods when a large number of members/visitors are present, i.e., opening day, July 4th, and Labor Day, are there any crowds to speak of. At the sign-in book next to the old flag pole, it is unusual to find more than five or six fishermen registered on a given day, other than those times mentioned above.

The second method of fishing Purdy's is the only other way to do so, and that is by becoming amphibious. Unless you are a duck, the most common ways of floating through the ranch are in a belly boat or a canoe, the former being by far the more popular of the two. When floating, the rules are clear, rigid and enforced. You are required to stay within the high water mark at all times, and on Silver Creek that generally means stay in the water, period. The float through Purdy's should be made with consideration of the ranch residents in mind; a simple matter of acting responsibly with courtesy and respect. A voyage through the entire ranch is an all-day summer thing; about six or seven hours. Some days, one hatch follows another and the long trip seems one hook-up after another. Great sport. Other days can be, as with all fly fishing places, hot, windy and very slow. These are reverently referred to as "Magellan Expeditions".

Sunny, wild daisies brighten a Fourth of July picnic on the Purdy Ranch below Kilpatrick Bridge.

Looking down from the Kilpatrick Bridge literally hundreds of very large trout may be observed any time of the year.

Consider too that the brew you had with lunch will usually work its way south within an hour or so and the rules being what they are...well, you figure that one out. So it is that many tubers choose to fish just the eastern extension of the pond below Kilpatrick Bridge, down to where a four-foot waterfall drops into the main channel, which continues on through the ranch. Working through this large piece of water, quite often alive with feeding trout, should occupy the better part of a fishing day.

If you should go to the far end of the pond, it's a good idea not to go over the falls. You probably wouldn't drown, but you most certainly would feel really dumb, and you would be disturbing the home of at least one monster brown that resides in the very deep pool below the falls.

The fish, nicknamed "Jaws", was caught, measured, photographed and released during the early summer of 1992. Angler: Dr. Steve Pauley, of Sun Valley, Idaho. Dr. Pauley was so moved by the encounter, he wrote the following passages, which appear here with his permission:

Starlight At Silver Creek

by Steve Pauley

I WAS TOLD THEY ONLY COME UP TO FEED ON DRY flies after dark, that they are huge fish, and only a few over 24 inches have ever been landed on dries.

This challenge was clearly spoken by many anglers who know Idaho's Silver Creek. In fact, I had tried many nights for many years, and had been broken off more times than I'll admit by these carnivorous, night stalking brown trout.

On this June night I had invited my friend Vince to join me and my regular fishing mentor, Rich, for an evening at Silver Creek. A nice PMD spinner fall occurred at 7:30 P.M. producing a few 16-inch rainbow and some smaller fish.

The usual lull before dark found us standing, waiting for the caddis to fill the air. Waiting for the big boys (and girls) that rise from the depths to feed on small children and other unsuspecting victims. Our job as brown trout night fighters was to protect and defend.

I had forgotten my fishing vest, (I qualify for the D.S. award at least weekly these days), so my options for tippet were limited. Since we had come to catch "Jaws", I decided to start with 4X-tippet and stay with it knowing that after dark I couldn't tie on anything new anyway. At sunset, when dusk produced a pink sky in warm breezes, I felt foolish throwing 4X-tippet on Silver Creek. Even 5X is scoffed at by both fish and angler for daytime fishing, but I knew if I ever hooked "Jaws", 4X would be a blessing.

After some slow fishing and two small browns on a No. 12 parachute caddis, I decided to commit to my

---

This is the pool directly below the little waterfall that drops from the big pond on Purdy Ranch. It is the residence of "Jaws" as described by Dr. Steve Pauley in "Starlight on Silver Creek."

Dr. Steve Pauley and his favorite brown trout "Jaws." The biggest fish taken on a dry fly for as long as most people can recall.

final night fly before it got too dark. I chose an Infrequens emerger, size 14. The reason for this is not clear since caddis were on the water. This particular Infrequens emerger is a custom-tie designed by Rich, and had always been a dynamite bug for all occasions. So why not use it tonight? As usual the fly you tie on at dark is the one you're stuck with until you hang it up for the evening or are broken off—which is usually the case. The large 4X-tippet was difficult to thread through the small No. 14 hook—especially with a near-dark sky.

The stars began to shine as a silhouette of Canadian Honkers moved in the western sky. Rich and Vince, fishing about 30 yards away, had caught two nice rainbow on parachute caddis. Suddenly I heard a large splash 15 yards to my left. I could see the remnants of a big swirl on the water. Was this Jaws?

My second cast in that direction produced another swirl in the region of my fly, which had long-ago become invisible on the darkening water. I was reacting to rises in the general area of my cast. When I reacted this time and raised my rod, it stopped short. I had a fish.

There was no jump. Just a very heavy pull that took my line first to the right, then left. I still didn't have the line on my Abel reel when I pressured the fish and began to realize just how heavy the tug was. I quickly got my line back on the reel. My Scott 10-foot/four-weight was bent further than I had ever seen it for such a consistent amount of time. Would it break?

Trusting (and praising) my 4X-tippet, I pressured the fish again, but it would barely budge. This fish was controlling me. I felt its head shake in long arcs as it swam slowly right and left, then deep, then toward me. I got a glimpse of its back and dorsal fin in the dark glare five feet in front of me. This is a big one. When it saw me it headed out again into the black water.

For 10 minutes it seemed I couldn't really move this fish anywhere. The bend in my four-weight was extreme. I called to Rich who had also seen the dorsal fin and was getting more interested in my predicament. "I think we may have a photo opportunity here, Rich," I said, my voice trembling slightly.

Vince brought his net over, and when I finally got the fish in close, it was obvious the net was way too small. "You couldn't beat this fish to death with that net, Steve. This fish is huge!", said Rich, who was now clearly very excited. His original estimate pegged it at 22 inches. (We estimate the familiar much more easily than the unknown and rarely-seen).

After a 20 minute battle the fish began to slowly relinquish it's home-water to the pull of my rod. My wrist was weakening from the constant heavy tug, but the adrenaline erased any thoughts of fatigue.

There it was, a huge female brown trout: Jaws! One of those giants we had been after for so long. A lifetime fish on a size 14 dry-fly. She measured 29 inches and weighed an estimated nine pounds. We marveled at her beauty in the starlight. Only the photographs would later show her colors. In the dark she seemed majestic, her spots almost invisible to our eyes.

I removed the fly from her upper lip, and after great consideration decided to release this trophy-brown. We all agreed to remain true to catch-and-release. The photos would be enough to recreate her later.

We kneeled in the shallow water with the fish at our thighs and nursed it back to strength. We measured her girth, felt her wide shoulders, and gazed at her pectorals. Her asymmetric tail spoke to years of wear from clearing gravel beds during spawning.

It was a magic moment. Three friends kneeling under starlight in Silver Creek on a warm summer night, with Jupiter bright in the west, and all three of us intent on reviving this wonderful creation of nature. I took note of the constellations: Scorpio, Leo, the Big Dipper. I felt a need to freeze-in-time the stars I know so well: Antares, Regulus, Arcturus, Vega, and Spica. I wished to savor it all; to remember the warm breezes, the pink sunset, the honkers, the rise, the set, the fight, the feel of her back, the laughter and the fun the three of us shared. And especially the release.

While fishing alone has its merits, moments like this need to be shared. We are born again. The world is right.

Caught Tuesday, June 23, 1992 10:20 P.M.
Story finished June 24, 1992 2:30 A.M.
(Couldn't sleep and had to write about it.)

Author's note:

It should be mentioned here that Steve Pauley is a medical doctor, not a professor of astronomy, although the stars and planets plainly share space in his knowledge-bank with eyes, ears, noses and throats. For those of us who flirt with this royal, piscatorial mistress called Silver Creek, it is gratifying to know that she does grant us her favor on rare occasions. Dr. Pauley has been so honored.

As guides working with clients on the creek like to say, "They're in there."

Another prudent tip when floating the pond between the bridge and the falls, would be to save enough energy and daylight to trudge your way back upstream to the bridge. Remember, you are still on private property and must remain in the water. Fins would help your propulsion, but tend to get sucked off your feet in the gunk.

The river from the Kilpatrick Bridge to Highway 20 is still Catch and Release, but single, barbless-hook lures are permitted as well as flies.

◆

Ron Lane displays a magnificent 22 inch brown taken on a No. 16 PMD in mid-June.

The Lower Water . . . Point Of Rocks . . . Old Larkin Ranch

BELOW THE HIGHWAY 20 CROSSING THE CREEK returns to areas of more public access and changes in physical character as it swings to the north for a distance of a couple of miles or so before resuming its eastward flow. Now drifting lazily through open meadow and into a dense willow grove, the stream is made to order for the big browns that lure fly rodders, spin fishermen and bait casters to the hunt. Still an excellent fly stream, it is now shared with trout fishermen of other persuasions.

This area is also an opportunity for those who don't feel as if they've been fishing unless they have something in the creel, to harvest a couple of trout for the evening meal. A slot limit of two fish, with all fish between 12 and 16 inches to be returned to the water immediately, is the current regulation. (See map: Silver Creek West)

As the river turns once more to the east there is more public access (See map: Silver Creek East) at a section of the stream known locally as "point of rocks". An extremely popular area, it is a haven for week-enders with RV's of all sorts. This section is to be avoided during opening week-

◆

Preceding page: The old Larkin Ranch just below Silver Creek East (Point-of-Rocks) public access area. This is where the brown drake hatch puts big fish on "ready alert" during early to mid June.

end if a quiet and reflective experience is your goal. Bud n' Velveeta camp here.

The lower stretch of Silver Creek does not rival the upstream runs when quantities of trout and swarming insect hatches are compared, but there is no shortage of large fish lurking in the shadows below the over-hanging willows and under the deeply-cut banks. On occasion, usually at dusk, a big brown cruiser may be seen chasing some swimming creature wildly about the shallows, mayhem on his mind. If the brown is truly hungry, as they are wont to be, he will consummate the chase favorably most of the time.

The biggest of the fish here are generally not very vulnerable to the fly fisherman's offerings simply because we can't cast a fly big enough for these voracious critters to become interested. A five to ten pound brown trout probably eats once or twice a day. When they are that size, they may eat whatever and whenever they damn-well please. The "what" may be a small fish, a baby duck, a mouse — a meal, not an appetizer. The "when" will likely be under the cover of darkness. These factors make the fly rodders quest all but impossible, except for a short period in early summer.

In late May to early June, this section of Silver Creek is the sight of an amazing natural phenomenon known as "The Brown Drake Hatch". When witnessed on the right day, at the peak-of-emergence, this hatch is forever inscribed in the memory of the dry fly buff. The adult brown drake is a huge bug. One of the largest mayflies of the genus, the body alone measures an inch or more in length. The hatch

◆

A typical summer day on the creek. Mornings are usually calm, but a stiff breeze often comes up about 1:00 or 2:00 p.m.

The Brown Drake, an early summer emerger, is a mouthful for trout, and a treat for Silver Creek fly anglers.

◆

starts downstream just before dark and wings it's way upstream in bomber formations of thousands at an altitude of twelve to fifteen feet off the water until reaching the willows, where it seems to dissipate. There are virtually no sightings of the insect above the highway bridge.

As darkness approaches, the duns and spinners cover the water and gulping trout become involved in a feasting orgy. It is the realization of mid-winter's night dreams. Only the coming of total darkness, when invisible flies are cast to invisible fish, impedes the festivities. Even then, casting to audible targets and striking audible rises continues into the cooling night. A classic game of "Pin-The-Tail...".

The brown drakes come off for about five to eight days, but the fish are more reckless in their feeding habits earlier in the occurrence. As the hatch progresses, it lessens in numbers and trout actually become quite selective, sometimes eating only duns and then only spinners or even nymphs. The type of dun preferred by the trout can also vary from day to day. One day a parachute works, the next it might be an extended-body or a cripple or emerger. No one ever said it was going to be easy.

Because the quarry is of such potential size, it may be assumed that 3X or 4X-tippet is called for during this show. Granted that the strength of such diameters would be comfortable, but unfortunately 5X draws more strikes. These are strong, healthy fish, as are all of the Silver Creek inhabitants. Enticing a rise and setting the hook are about the last duties performed by the fisherman for some time, the next several moments all belong to the fish. There is nothing to equal the complete and utter helplessness of watching the backing disappear from the spool of a screeching Hardy as a trout of unknown proportions heads toward Greater-Picabo like a run-a-way Peterbilt. The end of this scenario brings eerie silence as tippet and trout quietly part company some 150 yards downstream. The noisy reel is hushed. Then, the winding, the shaking and the laughter—or the cursing. The laughter is highly advised.

Should you be fortunate enough to be in attendance for all of the above, it is suggested you bring along a prayer book, a good attitude about getting "whupped", and if necessary your nitroglycerin pills. You'll likely need them all.

A short float below Point of Rocks brings us to an old and decrepit bridge shadowed by a large, solitary willow. A bona-fide Kodak "photo-op". This section is called the Old Larkin Ranch, and is private property carrying the same encroachment rules as Purdy's; you must stay in the water at all times. Why places are called by their former owner's names is a mystery. Perhaps it is easier to use a name that has been around awhile, rather than change it's name every time it changes ownership.

As this journal goes to press, fishing access may be obtained to Larkin's by paying a small, day-use-only, ranch fee. The fee is well worth the pittance paid when a day of serene privacy is hoped for—opening day for instance. Only four rods per day are currently allowed to fish the two and a half miles of Silver Creek that bisects the property, although floaters may slide through at any time. If the belly-boater is respectful of your water and glides quietly by, feeding fish will likely resume their activity within minutes after the transient passes.

From Larkin's the creek roams southeasterly through pasture and meadow, with little cover along the banks. The rancorous Princess seems to have mellowed slightly, her appearance now serene and less intimidating. Don't be deceived, she has merely changed her make-up. Fishing pressure is the lightest of the entire drainage here, with long, lonely runs of up to a mile available to floating fly fishermen who disdain crowds. No, there aren't the quantities of trout, nor the varied hatches that spice the preserve, but fishing can be excellent, and then there is that never-to-be-forgotten brown drake-thing early in the season. Some very knowledgeable Silver Creekers rate this as their favorite stretch when all is considered.

As we drift our canoe up to the grassy shore that marks the end of the odyssey, we can only guess how many trout we have covered in the many generative miles of river floated. The imagination marvels at the thought.

◆

Orange globe mallow is found along the streamside in early summer.

"The Hatches" . . . When They Happen . . . How To Fish Them

*T*HERE ARE DAYS WHEN JUST TOO DAMN MANY bugs are on the water. Here come Tricos, two kinds of Baetis, PMD duns and spinners, caddis and a few golden stones! The fish are going nuttso on one of them, hell, maybe two or more, but I'll be a son-of-a-buck if I can figure it out."

The above could well be a script handed out to all fly anglers as they sign-in at the Nature Conservancy cabin. Granted, it's not like this all the time, but the plot is not fictional in the least bit. It happens.

They're called "multiple hatches", and a lot of other names not nearly so descriptive nor complimentary. But rather than dealing with the negative aspect of too many insects, let us examine the very positive elements of the proliferation of trout food in this fish factory called Silver Creek.

Beginning with the opening of the general Idaho trout season on the fourth Saturday in May, and concluding with the close of the general season on the 30th of November, we'll look at each hatch as it occurs chronologically. The winter whitefish season, though not open on the Nature Conservancy, will also be addressed with regard to hatches and fishing methodology. Though casting to whitefish, few of this species are hooked by the hearty winter anglers. The great majority of fish "accidentally" caught during this frigid interlude are trout, which of course must be returned to the river unharmed at once.

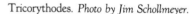

Tricorythodes. *Photo by Jim Schollmeyer.*

Late May can be a hit and miss affair on the Creek, depending upon what Mother Nature has in mind weatherwise. In 1992, El Niño brought an abnormally warm spring, with temps reaching into the 60's by March. As a result, all hatches in south-central Idaho were moved ahead by 10 days to two weeks. When the season opened on May 23rd, the brown drake hatch on the lower water burst forth with peak emergence, a full two weeks before normal. The hatches continued early for the balance of the summer. On the upper waters the pale morning duns (PMD's), another mayfly not often seen in abundance until early June, were on the water opening day. PMD's are a favorite of that generation of fly fishermen (45-plus) who can remember that Dwight David Eisenhower's favorite fly was the H and L variant. Even those with failing eyes can usually find a perky No. 16 PMD parachute bobbing along through a riffle next to the bubbles, naturals and a variety of other flotsam-and-jetsam.

The PMD has more to offer beyond being one of the easier hatches to see and to imitate; it is historically a late riser. Ordinarily this medium-sized fly will wait until the fly angler has had a second cup of coffee, read the sports page and leisurely made his way to the stream before making an appearance—say, no earlier than 10:00 A.M., often not until around noon. A decent and civilized hour by anyone's standards.

If the day is overcast and there has been a bit of drizzle, so much the better. The hatch may then continue unabated throughout the day, eventually diminishing late in the afternoon. An old bromide says something about "...bugs hatch and fish feed when the overall conditions are 'pleasant'". While most of us have had plenty of one-sided discussions with fish, usually questioning their parentage, scant few of us have ever had a two-sided conversation with one. Thus, we can't be absolutely certain what constitutes "pleasant". But we do know that coolish, humid days produce much better than hot, dry ones.

Fishing the PMD is first a matter of finding out, through trial and error, which of the several possible patterns the fish are interested in at the time. Are there only duns on the water? Spinners from the previous nights fall? Examine the water carefully, make your analysis and go from there, but don't be stubborn. If a No. 16 parachute dun doesn't bring some fish up, try a No. 18 thorax tie, or a no-hackle. If trout are obviously eating PMD-somethings, and they are ignoring your good presentations, change your fly after a dozen or two floats over rising fish. If they are just looking at your offering, or rolling short on it, put on a smaller size of the same pattern and reduce your tippet size. Silver Creek trout are historically selective, and he who triumphs must be creative and observant.

Presentation on most spring creeks is all-important and this spring creek is most definitely no exception. In fact, the PMD is the only fly that these fussy rascals will take when cast upstream to them, and that is not an always-thing.

The *Trico* and *Baetis* and *Calibaetis* almost always must be fished down and across or directly downstream. It's something about fish being leader/line shy. These trout live in Stoli-clear water. They have superb close-up vision. They see a whole lot of Dai-Riki tippets during the summer and they know the difference between a bug tied to 5X and one floating naturally, drag-free.

The PMD's hang around for a good part of the summer, but come mid-July, the bug-from-hell, the kissin' cousin of the No-See-Um, the favorite repast of all troutfish, the dread *Tricothyrodes*, ("Trico", if you please), appears in legion numbers on and over Silver Creek from one end to the other.

Inexplicably, this tiniest of mayflies creates a full-on, riotous feast by every Silver Creek trout not currently enrolled in Weight Watchers. When twenty or thirty large fish line up side-by-side, nose-to-tail, slurping thousands of Tricos at a sitting, fly fishermen must put an epithet on the whole happening; they call it a "Pod". How many of the wee creatures must be consumed by a twenty-inch trout to make a meal? A bunch.

Rookies, witnessing this binge for the first time, fumble with their equipment, drop their fly boxes, fall in the stream and generally come completely unglued as they eagerly prepare to reap a crop ripe to be harvested. Wrong. Foxy creek-vets know better. Listed below are an assortment of mistakes made by novices during the Trico eruption, and the accepted, though definitely not guaranteed, techniques employed by old hands:

(1) Casting upstream to fish. This was just covered a few casts back. Those who know fish straight downstream by using a stop cast, i.e., stopping the rod very high on the forward cast just to the side of the pod, dragging and re-aligning the fly three feet or so above the target(s), then lowering the rod tip slowly, allowing the fly to float to the fish naturally, leader and line upstream. This will also straighten the tippet. Finding your fly amidst the thousands of naturals is nigh impossible when a more typical up-and-across cast is made.

(2) Making long casts to fish in any direction. Not even the legendary Ted Williams, who it is said could read the logo on a fastball, could see a Trico spinner on the water at a distance of much more than ten feet, Superman could, with his Kryptonium lenses, at maybe 20 feet. Why then do mere mortals insist on double-hauling these pesky gnats? Use the down/across method described above and limit your casts to no more than 20 feet. The pod won't spook if you are careful in your approach and gentle with your

---

On a cool day in early fall, ideal conditions for Baetis, Earl Cohen makes down-and-across cast to surface feeder.

James K. Miller (the fourth, no less), a Silver Creek guide on a holiday "to get away from it all." Big brownie ate a Whitlock Hopper, measured 27 inches, estimated to weigh around seven pounds. A certified "pig." Photo by William McClannahan

◆

presentation. If you can find a good pair of Kryptonium glasses it wouldn't hurt either.

(3) Fishing with too large a fly and/or too heavy a tippet. Yes, you can sometimes take fish with a No. 16 parachute Adams when the menu dictates a No. 22 Trico. But if that doesn't work, you'll no doubt end up being forced to match-the-hatch more specifically, and that means at least by size, shape and shade - the three S's. During a No. 22 Trico hatch, a No. 22 parachute Adams just might be O.K. It is certainly the right size, the shape is pretty close and the dark body should be acceptable as well. What's more, it's a lot easier to see than a Trico-anything. Three or four feet of 6X-tippet tied to a 12-foot, 5X leader should be small enough, but stand ready to go to the "Angel Hair", 7X, if you get refusals.

A few more weapons for your Silver Creek arsenal:

The reach-mend cast has been discussed by many fly fishing notables over the past few years, and it is something that will be of much help in making the down-and-across drift so essential to taking fish at the Creek. The cast should be made at about a 45 degree angle downstream to the fish and about three feet or so above them. The reason the cast is aimed three feet above rather than the more conventional 12 to 18 inches, is to give you an opportunity to actually drag the fly to a drift line that is directly on line with the feeding target. When the Silver Creek trout are on an eating spree, they won't move very far to a natural, much less to an imitation. They simply don't have to expend that much energy, because the next bug will be along momentarily, right over their nose. It's cast, drag (i.e., correct), then release the fly (lower the rod tip slowly) allowing the fly to float directly over the feeding trout.

A small strike indicator affixed to the knot joining tippet to leader is a way to get some idea of where your fly is and therefore, a general area to search. On overcast days with glare, it is a chore to find even larger flies, nearly inconceivable to spot a No. 22 Blue Winged Olive or Trico. This will make it easier but not easy. If all else fails when fishing these teensy bugs, watch the strike indicator as you would when fishing a nymph. If the indicator hesitates at all, lift the rod tip quickly, but gingerly. This is not as exciting as watching the dry-take, but desperate men make desperate moves, and it still beats marshmallows.

Carry a couple of fine point permanent markers in a plastic baggie in your vest. One black and one brown should suffice. Often the BWO tied to match the *Baetis* hatch in progress will have a body that is too green or olive. Or maybe the hackle is too light. Streamside customizing with a permanent marker lightly dabbed on the body or wings or hackle may just be the trick to turn things your way. Apply sparingly or you'll end up with a black mess. The baggie should be the zip-lock type so that you won't have the only tie-dyed fly vest since 1968. There are no sure things in our sport, so none of the above chicanery will work all the time. We can only hope that some of these things fool some of the fish some of the time.

There are several species of *Baetis* inhabiting this system, among them *hagena* (formerly *parvus*). Some feel obliged to try to match the exact specie that is coming off. Others suspect that if an impostor of the correct size, shape and shade, not necessarily color, are close, and the presentation is perfect, the trout will be sufficiently conned.

This diminutive mayfly is the most maddening of the summer, as the trout doubtless key on them and sometimes will even pod-up on them. But the fish seem to know that the *Baetis* will be around for a while and they act indifferently to them. Whatever the reason, trout do not go berserko on this hatch as they do with Trico, or even PMD's. One day perhaps someone who was a trout in a former life will fill in some of the blanks for us. God knows there are some blanks.

◆

Mahogany Dun. Photo by Jim Schollmeyer

Callibaetis. *Photo by Jim Schollmeyer*

◆

The *Baetis* hatch is duped with a vast assortment of dries, emergers and nymphs. If the fish are obviously rising to duns, try a parachute BWO, a Slate/Olive no hackle or a local tie called the "Mason Loop-Wing", created by the Dean of Silver Creek guides and outfitters, Bill Mason. Mason moved to Sun Valley as the fly fishing boom of the seventies was dawning, and without a doubt has logged more hours on Silver Creek as a guide than anyone. Some thoughts he has on Loop-Wings, No-Hackles and Hatch-Matchers, deep, meaty stuff:

"When I came to Sun Valley in 1972, there were no official outfitters or guides. Bill Janss brought me here to make sure his Lodge guest/fly fishermen would get really professional instruction and direction. At the time, Dick Alf had the only fly shop in town, an amazing little place jammed floor-to-ceiling with rods, waders, boots—incredible. Dick also provided fly fishermen with the only fly most folks used on Silver Creek, the famous 'Hatch-Matcher'." The thought brings a chuckle from Mason before going on, "Imagine, one fly for Silver Creek. People used it during the Trico, Baetis, hell, anything that flew! No one knew what else to throw. I had been at the Henry's Fork during the late 60's-early 70's, when Doug Swisher and Carl Richards were putting together the first definitive work on spring creek bugs, Selective Trout, so I was privy to the latest in fly technology. 'No hackles', 'paraduns', 'emergers', and 'spinners' were totally foreign to all but a very few, mostly guys like Will Godfrey and Rene Harrop in the Henry's Fork area." A short break for a smoke, and the entomology lesson continued.

"The no hackle dun was really the first truly new innovation in flies since maybe hair-bodies. If you can find someone who can tie them right, they are deadly."

"My Loop-Wing was a child of necessity. Nothing we tried through the years did a very good job of mimicking the spent-wing of the Trico. When you look up at a Trico spinner floating on the water, its wings are clear, not white. Through trial and error we tried everything until finally I reasoned that maybe all that was needed was an outline of the wing. Bingo. That was about three years ago, and on the first ones I used 3X-tippet for the loop, which was too heavy. I now use 6X, and that works great. Because the fly is so doggone hard to see, I usually have people fish it directly into the sun, and look for just the definition on the surface, not really the fly."

During mid-summer there are additional bugs that never reach swarm-levels of emergence but are still of importance to the fly fisherman. The utmost of this group is the grasshopper. Were it not for insecticide control of these insects, there probably would be heavier concentrations, as the creek runs through prime hopper country. But the

◆

Nature film maker Jim Dutcher with handsome Silver Creek rainbow taken at the Kilpatrick Bridge.

Author releases 20 inch rainbow fooled by a No. 20 BWO parachute tied to 7X tippet. Photo by Ken Tsukihara.

farmer and the fly fisherman have contrary objectives with regard to the hopper. Farmers look upon the lowly bugs as eating machines, and they are eating his crops, consequently his money. The fly angler sees the hopper as a tasty morsel for large trout, an invitation to success. The farmer usually wins this one, but on stretches of Silver Creek there are native environs where no crops exist, and here hoppers will still be found. It is in these locations that the fly rodder is advised to plop a juicy Whitlock Hopper hard to the bank and be prepared for a violent rise from fish as far away as six feet. Beetles and ants too, can dredge up trout from their August doldrums when floated through riffles or fished in the scum.

As the days grow shorter and nights cooler, the fisherman's golden season approaches. Wildflowers fade, and green aspens metamorphose as the brilliant hues of autumn glow vividly along the river and high on the neighboring hills. Hemingway wrote as a eulogy, in part, for his departed hunting mate, Gene Van Guilder, "...Best of all, he loved the fall." He was not alone.

Sluggish grasshoppers no longer rocket from the pathways to the Creek. Frost greets early morning anglers, and squawking mallards and geese announce their arrival from the north. The short, glorious summer will soon be gone. These are the days to cherish. Pleasant temperatures, wispy, cloud-streaked skies and nearly-deserted stretches of prime water on which to seek targets of opportunity are the special gifts of September.

Preceding page: California visitor John Bonk casts to feeding fish on a lovely July day. This is the old Larkin Ranch water.

In the early fall the sprightly Calibaetis appears, to fill the afternoons with free-rising fish. Dancing gaily above the creek, the Calibaetis, or Speckled Spinner, is a welcomed sight after two months of straining the eyes on Trico and Baetis.

Not that the Calibaetis is a huge fly—it is rarely imitated with anything larger than a No. 16, more often a No. 18. But flies that size floating in the slick backwaters and eddies look like an America's Cup regatta in comparison to the flies of hatches recently passed.

The mayfly duns will commence their yo-yo gyrations from around noon until as late as 2:OO P.M., depending on the whims of the weather. Freshly-hatched duns dot the surface, floating as tiny sailboats temptingly on the water,

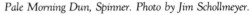

Pale Morning Dun, Spinner. Photo by Jim Schollmeyer.

wings fluttering slightly, all but begging trout to come and eat. The trout are cooperative, at times moving swiftly though shallow, calm water sucking in dun after dun in an omnivorous, eating rampage. When fish are involved in this kind of foraging, it no longer resembles the rhythmic, dimpling rise form of a limestone trout delicately sipping naturals somewhere south of Chelsea-by-Avon. No, these are big Idaho trout, lustfully absorbed in the ingestion of a generous midday meal. These fish are also vulnerable to the fly casters offerings during this period. The game now becomes one of chance. The fish seldom reveal a pattern when taking the duns, but move in all directions, wherever a bite is waiting—the "Great Whites" of Silver Creek.

If and when they do eat your fly, it is a sudden act, almost unexpected, without much concern for tippet size or ceremony. Your fly must be a close replica of those on the menu, however. These fish have no jobs, no hobbies, no other interests. They just swim and eat, and they are quite accomplished at both. Since swimming is a natural thing, they really need pay attention to just the one occupation, that of being professional gluttons. Bon appetit.

Both duns and spinners are on the water simultaneously, as with the PMD's, and fish can be extremely selective in their preference. Starting out with a parachute tie or a thorax pattern, and then pinch-hitting with the harder-to-see spinner would be the likely batting order. There is usually no question about what fly the fish are taking at this time of year. Even if Baetis are coming off simultaneously, the fish will probably prefer the *Calibaetis*. Then it becomes a matter of merely establishing which pattern, what size, etc. The "merely" can be much easier said than done some days.

It is when writing of hatches and the ways of trout, that one wonders how authors would approach the subject without the use of cover-your-butt discourse such as "usually", "probably", "sometimes", "normally" and "maybe". If objectivity without hedging were the rule, few words about fly fishing would be written. That is an absolute—for a change.

When the frost is on the Halloween pumpkin, and the fly line freezes in the guides, the season for the dry fly purist is drawing to an end. River life is quiet. Gutsy little *Baetis* still make sporadic showings, but the summer intensities are long gone. Now is the time for "chuck and duck".

Autumn's blaze signals the commencement of the annual brown trout spawning period on Silver Creek, and the opportunity to do battle with some truly sizable fish. This is far from the fine and sensitive dry fly experience of the Trico emergence.

Put the four-weight rod in the closet along with the 7X and box of wimpy little flies. These fish are the trout-world's counterparts of offensive linemen in the NFL.

Ephemerella Inermis (Pale Morning Dun). Photo by Jim Schollmeyer

They want meat and potatoes and plenty of both. Translated to fish language, this means a No. 8 Woolly Bugger complete with sparkle-trim and perhaps beady-eyes, tied to a nine-foot leader with 3X or 4X tippet. Gasp! It's enough to make Dame Juliana Berners roll over in her Vault-on-the-Test. Trout, however, have no sense of purity. They sense only a bonny chance to devour another savory morsel. When they do, there is nothing subtle about the take, and the fight is joined resolutely.

The chill of Thanksgiving is a reminder that it will be six dark months before the stream awakens and once again repeats its perpetual cycle. For now, only the microscopic midges, or chironomids, are left to endure the winter and bring trout to visible life. Incredibly, the constant temperatures of the spring creek keeps the water from freezing, and trout continue to rise throughout the entire length of the river. After the close of the general season the Silver Creek Preserve closes until May, but the statewide whitefish season remains open on all other water through March. Float-tubes will be found bobbing about the pond area below Kilpatrick Bridge for the balance of the winter. Sitting in the "donuts" will be half-crazed, half-frozen fly fishermen, often grinning ear-to-ear, rods-bent in an inverted U, fast to a trout of some size. These anglers are clinically sane. They are doctors, mothers, carpenters, lawyers, priests, bartenders—all reasonably normal humans with but one warped flaw, a passion for this thing called fly fishing. Pity them.

◆

Wild, lavender aster dots the hills above the steam in August.

The Grand Lady Of Silver Creek . . . And Others

IN JANUARY OF 1937, TWO WEEKS AFTER THE "SWELL" new ski resort of Sun Valley, Idaho celebrated its holiday opening, a petite young lady from Chicago traveled more than 1500 miles by rail to do some day-schussing and night-shuffling. For the youthful and athletic Clara Spiegel, 32, the rest was history.

So impressed was she by the high peaks, charming valley and tumbling river running through town that she could scarcely wait to come back in the summer. She returned to find a vista even more lovely than the snow-covered land she had discovered in the winter. It was the beginning of a lifelong love affair that continues today.

Although Clara isn't certain whether she fished that first summer, she remembers well getting her indoctrination into fly casting/fishing from Sun Valley's chief fishing guide, Taylor Williams, during the summer of 1938.

"Taylor was a masterful caster, and fisherman," reflected Clara one snowy November afternoon in her Ketchum home, "and a terrific guide as well."

"He would get so excited when I hooked a good fish, and there were so many trout in those days, the only way you wouldn't catch fish would be if you simply couldn't cast a lick or you fell headlong into them (the fish) in the river."

"In those naive days of 1938, there were so few fishermen and so much open water, crowds as we know them today were unimaginable," she continued. Clara Spiegel tells of another man who guided her on the creek "...sometime back then."

"Don Anderson was a big man, and he always insisted that I wear a large belt, snugged waist-high around my chest-waders. When we went into the water, Don would have one of his large and strong hands wrapped around the belt at my back. If I ever slipped or got a bit stuck, he would just lift me up out of the stream with that strong arm of his."

After casting flies for 54 years on Silver Creek, what is Clara's biggest fish?

"I'm glad you asked," she answers spryly, digging into an envelope for a photo she had intended to reveal all along.

"Twenty-five and a half inches, measured," she says with a spark in her voice and a glint in her eyes, "and at least six-and-a half pounds, according to Bud Purdy, who was there!"

The photo shows an enormous male brown trout, flush with spawning colors, gold and brown and red and noble, being held by a special little 87-year-old lady from Ketchum, Idaho. Make that, being proudly displayed by The Grand Matron of Silver Creek, Clara Spiegel.

Was this a picture from the thirties or forties perhaps?

"Why, absolutely not", the angler protests, "took him three weeks ago (October, 1992)."

Places To Stay . . . Where To Eat
What To Do . . . How To Come

Cheers! Mary Ann Charles displays the ultimate in beginners luck: A 19-inch brown on the first day of fly fishing.

◆

There are no records kept for such things, but one can only wonder how many bigger fish have ever been taken on a fly rod by an 87 year-old. The guess would be not many.

On the same day Clara landed her personal best, her guest for the day, Mary Ann Charles, on her very first fly fishing outing, caught and released a 19-inch-brown estimated to weigh around three-and-a-half pounds. Apparently no one told her that was impossible. Eat your hearts out boys.

When "The Colonel", Taylor Williams, died in 1959, the Silver Creek fishing guide line up was mostly assembled from European-born ski instructors who knew how to get to the Creek and not a whole lot more. An exception to that was legendary Sepp Froehlich. Sepp was a splendid fly fisherman and became famous for his cookouts on the stream. Thinning the herd of a few trout probably didn't hurt the fishery much then, and guests thoroughly enjoyed the stream-to-the-skillet meals, which always included Sepp's famous potatoes. Sepp was also known to slip away from his clients periodically to throw a few flies himself.

The good old days were pretty good. But now isn't all that bad, and tomorrow looks even better. We may be stuck with the crowds, and as a result the trout will surely be wiser and even more niggling. Would we have it any other way? Probably not.

THOSE AMONG US WHO TRAVEL THE WEST IN SEARCH of rivers and bugs and wild trout often find that at our journeys-end the terms "lodging" and "dining" have been stretched to the furthest extent of advertising license. Rarely do great trout waters run through artsy little crossroads featuring patio dining and menus of stir-fried scallops with fresh garden vegetables or medallions of veal in a beurre blanc. Suffice to say, that the allure of the excursion is not the room, nor the board.

Most trout streams are far from the path of those who place eating fine foods and sleeping in regal surroundings high on their list of priorities, thankfully. The majority of these waters are to be found near hamlets that might best be described as "unique", or "friendly"—places like Craig, Montana (Missouri River headquarters), where the Cafe-Bar serves up whiskey, Coors, homemade Polish sausage, pickled-pigs-feet, pickled eggs and Joe's-special-chili, all chock-full of calories, salt, fat and mucho cholesterol. But one is not limited to that bill of fare by any means. No sir. Right across the street, bean and cheese burritos, chorizo tamales, Hobos and pepperoni pizza are yours for the asking in the blinding flash of microwave minutes.

Now, when the "boys" are on a road trip to one of these quaint river hide-aways, they can tolerate, perhaps almost enjoy this diet for a couple of days. But for a week or two? No way. Unless you are part coyote, your stomach will cry "No mas!".

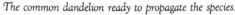

◆

The common dandelion ready to propagate the species.

Excellent, deep pool right at the road holds some huge fish.

♦

That's one of the reasons Silver Creek is the perfect retreat for any fly fisherman with "baggage", whether that includes a husband, wife, kids, in-laws or your Aunt Millie. With the exception of those camping-out in a tent or driving their own motel, visitors will probably opt to stay in the sister ski-resort towns of Ketchum/Sun Valley, some 25-30 miles north of the Creek. This is no Dutch John, Utah; Hardin, Montana; or Pinedale, Wyoming. Nor could it ever be likened to that picturesque core of Epicurean delight, Blanco, New Mexico on the San Juan River.

Because skiers like to eat well and stay in nice places, Sun Valley (we'll just call the whole area Sun Valley for simplification, though many of the establishments listed are in Ketchum) is loaded with excellent lodging, and a tasty assortment of restaurants, all comfortably removed from the Creek. Also, remember that Averill Harriman wanted plenty of things for people to do in the summer to entice guests to stay in his lodge. So he built a golf course in the Trail Creek valley behind the lodge, snug to the little stream that wanders menacingly along the fairways and through the village. The Sun Valley Golf Course is ranked by most golf directories as one of the top 100 resort courses in the country. Neighboring Elkhorn, a resort within a resort, also features an outstanding 18 hole championship layout. There are two nine hole courses in the area as well – Warm Springs and Bigwood. All are open to the public.

If golf isn't what Aunt Millie had in mind, there are dozens of tennis courts, miles of hiking and biking trails, horseback riding, rollerblading, white-water raft trips, glider flights and enough photo possibilities to fill a National Geographic. There is also lake/spin-bait-fishing just for kids, river fishing for everyone, and free fly-casting clinics four nights a week all summer long, put on by the various outfitters in town. That ought to keep Millie out of the bars.

But a word of caution; if you are trying to shed a few pounds, this is not a good place to be. There are no less than 65 restaurants (and counting) in the Sun Valley/Ketchum confines, including:
($-inexpensive $$-moderate $$$-expensive $$$$-very)

Mexican food: Desperado's and Mama Inez. $
Italian/pizza: Louie's, Rico's, Smokey Mountain. $
Steak and chop houses: Pioneer Saloon, Sawtooth Club, Ketchurn Grill, Warm Springs Ranch, Ore House, Jesse's. $$

Italian/pastas: Piccolo, Salvatore's, Baldy Base Club $$

Continental cuisine: Chez Michel, A Matter of Taste, Mango, Peter's, Creekside. $$$

Elegant Dining: Evergreen, The Lodge Dining Room, Epitome, Soupcon, Christiania. $$$$

Morning Food/Lunch: Perry's, The Kitchen, The Kneadery, The Buffalo Cafe, Java on Main, Grumpy's. $

Oriental: China Pepper, Globus Noodle, Can Tho, Panda. $$

If you can't find something to satisfy your appetite here, you aren't in the least bit hungry.

Fishing Silver Creek and staying in Sun Valley offers the fly fisherman and friends or family that rare opportunity to enjoy not only the fishing, but the apres-fishing as well. While some members of the party are plying the slick waters of the Creek, those who follow other pursuits may partake in any of the previously listed athletic endeavors, or browse through the considerable number of shops scattered in and around Ketchum and Sun Valley. Everything from Polo to Pendleton may be found here, including the largest year-around Christmas shop between Idaho and Bavaria.

If art is your thing, then let Dad fish till the cows come home, you'll have plenty of local and nationally recognized artist's work to peruse. No less than 23 galleries, including photo, artifacts and glassworks, are listed in the Yellow Pages of the local phone book.

All summer long the Sun Valley Ice Rink, made famous by Sonja Henie in the 1941 motion picture, "Sun Valley Serenade", serves up the very best in skating entertainment, featuring the world's top skaters. Recent performers include Katarina Witt, Scott Hamilton, Brian Boitano, Brian Orser and Linda Fratianne. The shows run weekly from June through September.

Another highlight of the summer is the staging of outdoor musical performances presented by Sun Valley Center for the Arts and Humanities. Among those productions seen of late were, Emmy Lou Harris, Herbie Mann, the Dallas Brass, and the Utah Symphony.

Still haven't hit your hot button? Well then, how about ballet? The annual "Summerdance" in Elkhorn is recognized nation-wide as one of the top productions of its kind, attracting star talent from all over the globe. This is a week-long affair in mid-summer.

◆

The creek below Highway 20.

For the exploring types there are ghost towns or remnants of what once were ghost towns, at Boulder City (near the location of the Clint Eastwood movie, "Pale Rider") and Bonanza, an hour and a half drive away, through the awesome Stanley basin. On the latter excursion you'll follow the headwaters of the Salmon River, which at this point, is not so mighty. Your route will also parallel the rugged peaks of the Sawtooth Mountain Range to the west and the White Clouds to the east. Near Bonanza is the immense barge floated up the Yankee Fork of the Salmon to dredge for riches as recently as 40 years ago. The ravaged river bed is a grim reminder of what destruction man is capable of when left to his own devices and greed.

About 30 miles east of Silver Creek on Highway 20, lies a natural curiosity called Craters of the Moon National Monument. This bizarre landscape so nearly resembles that of the moon, that NASA trained our lunar astronauts here. It is well worth a visit.

———————————◆———————————

Clara Spiegel, 87 years young, hefting her mammoth brown trout taken on the Purdy Ranch in October of 1992. Quite amazing.

Transportation: One of the very few knocks aimed at the magnificent destination ski resort of Sun Valley, Idaho, has always been that "you can't get there from here." Since the Sun Valley area is the closest town of any size to Silver Creek, the same might be said about getting there to fish. But skiers are spoiled, and though air connections aren't great, fly fishermen are accustomed to much worse. Consider getting to the Big Horn, or Hat Creek or even the Madison. And, there have been substantial improvements in both frequency and choice of airlines in recent years. Friedman Memorial Airport in Hailey, 14 miles south of Ketchum, is served by Horizon Air (Alaska Airlines) and Sky West (Delta Airlines). Alaska serves all of the West, including Seattle, San Francisco and Los Angeles, and Delta connects via Salt Lake to the rest of the country. Another option might be to fly into Boise via United or the above carriers then rent a car and drive the two and a half hours to the Ketchum/Sun Valley area. Most major car rental companies are represented in Boise and Hailey.

If you are driving, Sun Valley is about 10 driving hours north of Las Vegas, Nevada on U.S. 93 (connecting with Idaho 75 in Shoshone, Idaho); five to six hours northwest of Salt Lake City via I-15 to just below the Idaho border then west on I-84 (Idaho's only east-west interstate) to Twin Falls and then north for approximately 70 miles on U.S. 93. From the north (Calgary, Missoula), follow U.S. 93 south to Challis, veer to the west on Idaho 75 and cling precipitously to the edge of the Salmon River as it winds via the town of Stanley with the rugged Sawtooth Mountains on your right. Continue up over Galena Summit and down into the Wood River Valley and the headwaters of the Big Wood River for twenty five miles or so to Ketchum.

Lodging Accommodations: Because this area houses thousands of skiers each winter, there is a wide range of rental housing from quite inexpensive motels to grand riverfront homes. Property management contacts: Alpine 800 251-3037 Mountain Resorts at Sun Valley 800 635-4444 Resort Reservations 800 635-8242 Peak Investment Properties 800 245-8443

The area also boasts a very nice RV park, Sun Valley RV Resort, (208) 726-3420; right on the Big Wood River just a mile or so south of Ketchum. In addition, there are excellent "rough" camping facilities scattered along the Big Wood River to the north of Ketchum, all within an hours drive of Silver Creek. For locations, contact the Sawtooth National Recreation Area HQ.

Outfitters, Guides And Fly Shops: (listed alphabetically) Lost River Outfitters: (next to Boulder Mountain Village) 620 N. Main (Hwy 75), Ketchum, (208) 726-1706, Complete fly shop, 14 guides; Bill Mason Oufitters: (on the Sun Valley Mall) (208) 622-9305, Complete fly shop, 8 guides; Silver Creek Outfitters: 507 N.

Main (Hwy 75), Ketchum, (208) 726-5282. Complete fly shop, 20 guides; Sun Valley Outfitters: (in the Colonnade, Sun Valley Road) (208) 622-3400, Complete fly shop, 6 guides.

The Tackle Bag: Any fly rod between eight feet and nine feet throwing a line of 4-5-6 will be satisfactory, although the higher end of those numbers, a 9-foot/6-weight, will make casting easier if (when?) the wind picks up, and for chucking those big Woolly Buggers in the fall. For those who fish nymphs, a floating line is usually all that is needed on the Creek. To get a nymph down deeper, a small split shot affixed to the leader about four to six inches from the fly is the procedure used by most guides. If the fish are taking emergers, a floater with no weight on the leader will let the fly work just under the surface. Also, the use of a strike indicator placed 18-36 inches or so up from your emerger pattern will greatly aid in seeing those subtle, invisible takes. Make sure of good dry fly presentations by keeping your fly line clean and floating high.

What To Wear/Weather: As with any Rocky Mountain locale, go prepared for a mixed bag of weather. May can be downright chilly. June is sometimes cool with thundershowers. Ditto the sudden downpours in July and August, but temperatures are generally quite warm. September is the favored month by regulars who know from past history that the main body of tourists are gone and the days are cooler, clear and comfortable. Nights are somewhat more than crisp, try the low thirties-high twenties. October usually brings snow and November always does, therefore unless you are a descendant of Grizzly Adams, be forewarned, dress warmly! Neoprene waders are highly suggested all year. They will be warm in mid-summer, but they are just much more maneuverable, comfortable, and safe (and don't forget the leeches). It's always a good idea to stick a light rain jacket or nylon wind breaker in the back of your vest for those unscheduled showers previously mentioned. Long sleeved shirts are prudent as well. They will keep the sun from baking your arms, keep bugs from eating you, keep you warmer if the weather changes suddenly, and they can always be rolled up if it's just too dang hot. Polarized sun glasses are an absolute must! You can't set the hook if you can't see the fly. A baseball cap, visor or any hat that has a wide brim should also be worn on the stream. The brim will keep the sun off your face and will greatly improve your visions of delicate rises, your floating fly, and the strike.

◆

Thanksgiving Day means only days remain in the regular fishing season on the Nature Conservancy water. Dress warmly.

Photo Jim Schollmeyer.

Suggested Fly Patterns

Whitlock's Hopper. A super fly in July and August when the weather is warm and the afternoon breezes have blown the smaller mayflies and caddis off the water. Fish tight to the banks on the windward side of the stream. Sizes: No. 8 to No. 14.

Black Beetle. Another pattern that will take fish when others fail. Fish this bug also on the windward side of the stream against the bank. Beetles tied with a bit of fluorescent tag on top will be much easier to see. Sizes: No. 14 to No. 18.

Flying Black Ant. The third of the three "Windy Wonders". Most Silver Creek patterns of this ant are tied with white wings and are somewhat easy to see. The ant may be fished against the bank or drifted through a riffle. Sizes: No. 14 to No. 18.

Pale Morning Dun (PMD). PMD's are fun to fish because they are usually a late morning riser, allowing the angler to enjoy an extra cup of coffee in the morning before assaulting the creek. And, it is the easiest to see. Sizes: No. 14 to No. 22.

Trico (*Tricorythodes*). The largest member of the "no-see-um" family, which makes it just larger than an amoeba. Big fish absolutely love these little bugs, inhaling thousands of them at each meal. Now, which one is yours? Sizes: No. 20 to No. 22.

Mahogany Dun. Generally not an abundant hatch in sheer numbers, but a factor nevertheless when they are on the water. Difficult to see due to coloration – what's new? Fish this fly in the seam between fast and slow water. Sizes: No. 16 to No. 20.

Tan/Olive Slate Wing No-Hackle. Imitates a number of mayflies, including *Baetis, Calibaetis* and PMD. Very realistic appearance on water, but the wings tend to split after a few minutes of casting or a couple of fish. Sizes: No. 18 to No. 22.

Baetis (Parachute). Easiest of all *Baetis* patterns to see. Translation: If you have good eyes you can see it clearly to a distance of say, six feet. Unfortunately, no self-respecting trout will be closer than 20 feet away. Sizes: No. 18 to No. 22.

Baetis (3/4 spent). This little guy is a killer when floated drag-free over feeding fish during the many Silver Creek *Baetis* hatches. The smaller of these flies are best fished with 6X or 7X. Guess what? Hard to see. Sizes: No. 18 to No. 22.

Calibaetis (Dun). Early afternoons in August/September bring these bouncy rascals out in great numbers and the big bows and browns of Silver Creek savor them. The duns look like little sailboats in the ponds and slicks. Sizes: No. 16 to No. 20.

Calibaetis (Spinner). Sometimes, even when there are duns on the water, fish ignore them completely, but for some reason they will eat the spinners big time. Don't ask me. Ask the silly fish why they do what they do. Sizes: No. 16 to No. 18.

Brown Drake. This huge mayfly is present only on the lower reaches of the creek, in slower water near Picabo. They are significant however, because when they appear, they provide a feast for large trout. Mid-June hatch. Sizes: No. 6 to No. 12.

Parachute Adams. Probably the single most popular fly used on Silver Creek. The smaller sizes could imitate *Baetis*, Trico or caddis, but my guess is that this most favored of all flies just floats right, looks buggy, is easy to see, and it works! Sizes: No. 16 to No. 22.

Brassie (Nymph). Some say the very best way to take selective trout in spring creeks. Likely represents many aquatic nymphal and larval stages. Fish with floating line, fine tippet, no weight, strike indicator, in film. Sizes: No. 18 to No. 22.

Woolly Bugger. Here we have possibly the ugliest fly created by fly tiers since this whole thing began centuries ago. Attila the Hun would have fished with this fly, and he would have caught huge browns with it in the fall. Sizes: No. 6 to No. 10.

Quite obviously, this is only a suggested list of flies to be tried on Silver Creek. Some days none of them will work, other days you might keep a Parachute Adams on all day long. One never knows when dealing with these slip-

pery creatures. Maybe that's why it's called "fishing", not "catching". Most of us carry an additional 80 to 90 patterns in our vests, just in case.

There are also a great many variations to these basics, i.e., Steve Pauley's favored Infrequens emerger and Bill Mason's Loop-Wing, and even Dick Alf's Hatch-Matcher. The list can be as long as your 7X-tippet during the Trico hatch. Generally, the best rule is to fish flies with which you have confidence. If you aren't pretty sure you're going to be successful with your choices, you probably won't be. If you can't solve the puzzle of what fly is hot, all of the fly shop/outfitters in town will be able to furnish you with current, daily data on the Flies du Jour, and fill any voids you may have in your box.

Now that your vest pockets are loaded with enough flies to open a small shop, make room for a couple more items that are really needed. Sun Valley is at an altitude of approximately 6,000 feet and Silver Creek is only about 1,500 feet lower, so the sun's rays can be deadly. No matter how well-tanned you may be, it just doesn't make good sense to be out on a trout stream any time of the year without sunscreen – at least SPF 15 – on all your exposed parts. The other item to have handy is insect repellent. Depending upon how wet the spring has been, mosquitoes can be merely a nuisance, or a real pain in the neck and elsewhere. June and July are the worst months for these pests on Silver Creek, but they can also be around in May if the spring is warm and August if the summer is rainy.

If you plan a full day on the Creek, you are advised to take along a cooler with sandwiches and liquid refreshments. There are no McDonald's nearby, thank goodness, and the general store in Picabo offers bologna, beer and bread, not much more.

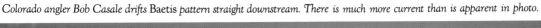

Colorado angler Bob Casale drifts Baetis *pattern straight downstream. There is much more current than is apparent in photo.*

Hendrickson Thorax   Parachute Adams   Callibaetis Dun   Callibaetis Spinner
Mahogany Dun   Baetis 3/4 Spent   Baetis Parachute Trico   Brassie
Pale Morning Dun   Pale Morning Dun (Cut Wing)   Slate Olive   Tan Olive
Brown Drake   Whitlock Hopper
Woolly Bugger   Black Beetle   Black Flying Ant

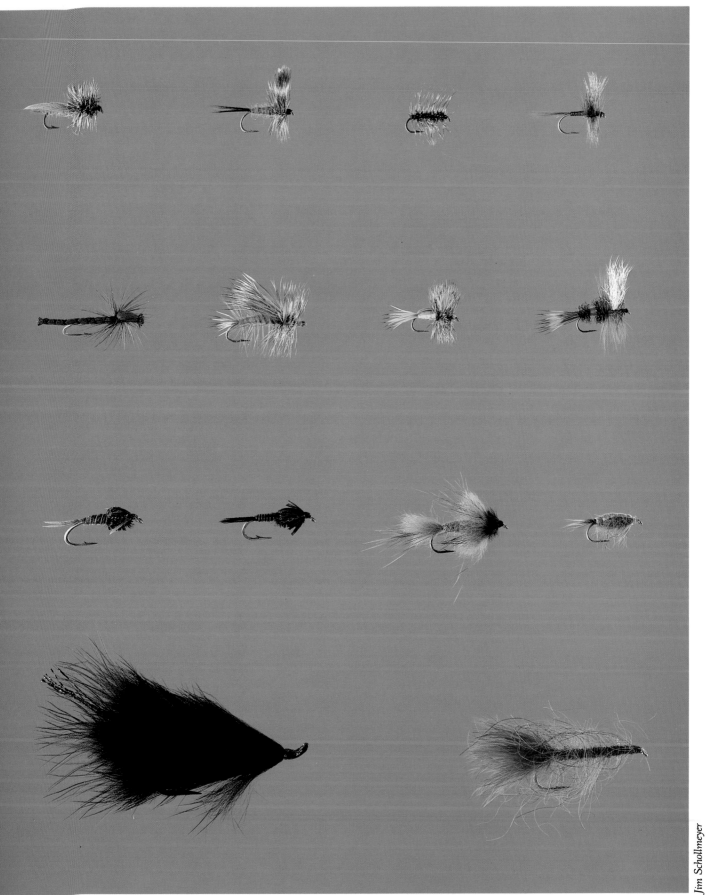

Low Water Hemingway Caddis   Standard Adams   Griffith Gnat   Quill Gordon

Blue Damsel   Kaufmann Stimulator   Lime Humpy   Royal Wulff

Standard Pheasant Tail   Dark Olive Pheasant Tail   Casual Dress   Olive Scud

Black Bunny Leech   Brown Mohair Leech

Personal Reflections Of A Devout Addict

AFTER COMPLETING THE MAIN BODY OF THIS JOURnal, it occurred to me that maybe I've made fishing Silver Creek seem too onerous a task for fly fishermen with even better-than-average skills. But after reviewing my work, I am reluctant to say that the word-picture I've painted is pretty much the way it is. The fish are finicky and stubborn. The hatches are maddening. The currents are confounding. The wind is often brisk and surly.

Why then do I get in line along with so many others to be so rudely and summarily thrashed? Is this the ultimate masochistic ritual of intimidation by a far-lesser life form, the lowly trout?

I hope you are not expecting me to shed profound and brilliant light on these questions. My objective here is to pose and ponder, to ignite a spark within your thought processes so that your way will be clear. Then, when you stand on the stream bank in the freezing cold, thoroughly whipped, hungry, wet and frazzled, you will know one thing: bowling might warrant some further consideration as a more sensible pastime.

◆

Between Loving Creek and S-Turn on a glassy autumn afternoon.

Bill Mason, who should know, says flatly, "I've been about everywhere trout live. New Zealand, Argentina, Alaska and all over the homeland; Silver Creek is absolutely the most demanding piece of water I have ever fished. Period."

So about 7,000 times a year on the Silver Creek Preserve alone, tenacious people with fly rods and presumably little in the way of good sense, flail away at a trout population resolved to ignore most attempts to deceive them. The great majority of these anglers know full well what they are getting into before they make the first cast, yours truly included. Call it the lure of the challenge, the thrill of the contest, the anticipation of the conquest, whatever. The sparkling waters of this silvery creek attract us like the spider's web attracts the moth. We are incurable addicts; we admit it and love it.

Were this place always totally impossible, it likely would not have the magnetism it has; even boldly optimistic fly anglers can usually differentiate between the difficult and the hopeless. Every once in a great while, the fish goddess of Silver Creek smiles upon us and makes the rising and taking of fish almost easy. On back-to-back days recently, I fished from a tube above Kilpatrick Bridge. On the first day I took ten handsome rainbows in a matter of slightly more than two hours. All trout were seduced by a No. 16 Parachute Adams. The fish taped at 12 to 17 inches. The following day, almost identical to the day previous, using the same exact fly and fishing in different runs of the same general area, I drew the Platinum Bagel...zip...zero...nada. How had I offended them? Was I too taken by my new-found glories? Irreverent perhaps? As soon as we find that someone who lived previously as a trout, I'll ask him about that day and several others that were much the same.

The Platinum Bagel, by the way, is awarded to Silver Creek anglers more frequently than the Good Conduct Medal is awarded to our fighting men in uniform. If each recipient of this ignoble acclaim were recorded in one grand edition, it would surely be among the thickest books in the library. All names chronicled end-to-end would stretch from Picabo to Pocatello and back. To wear the "PB" is to show the angling world that you are humble, deserving, dedicated and not too irascible. My own personal laurel is festooned with many oak-leaf clusters, symbolic of numerous repeat presentations.

Despite all of the above, I shall always return for more, for I can think of no other place that soothes as it rankles me, crushes yet caresses me, and no place I hold higher. Times spent on Silver Creek are mercifully not measured by fish count. They are gauged by the hours spent wading the currents, reveling in the surroundings and relishing the whole, in spite of the sometimes agonizing parts.

I am awed by the enigma of such a paradox. I am a devoted, eternal subject of her Highness, the Creek of Silver.